BOLOGNA

ILLUSTRATED
TOURIST GUIDE

Realizzazione Tanieli Antonio - Imola

© **STUDIO FARO**, Santovito Alberto
BOLOGNA

MANAGING DIRECTOR: SANTOVITO ALBERTO
PERIODICAL: PIANTE TOPOGRAFICHE D'ITALIA
AUTHORIZATION NUMBER NR. 4702; 22 JANUARY 1979

PRINTED ON 10-2013: VISUAL PROJECT soc.coop. - Zola Predosa (BO)
TEXT WRITTEN BY FABRIZIO CORSINI DEL MONTE
PHOTOGRAPHER: PAOLO VECCHI
TRANSLATED BY ANNALISA ORLANDI

INDEX

View of the Exhibition neighbourhood; modern towers built by the Japanese Architect Kenzo Tange

GENERAL INFORMATION

Bologna, chief town of the Italian region Emilia Romagna, is located between the two rivers Reno and Savena in the Po Valley (Pianura Padana), backing the Apennine Tosco-Emiliano. The town has a population of about 410,000, an altitude above sea level of 54 metres and an area of 140,000 square km. This peculiar geographical location makes Bologna an important centre for the promotion and the development of both domestic and international economy of Italy. This being the case, many of well-known European Exhibitions are held yearly at the FIERA DISTRICT, a business area designed by the Japanese architect Kenzo Tange.

Airport G.Marconi: Departures

In addition to being reputed to possess the most ancient University in all Europe and, therefore being called *"La Dotta"* (erudite), Bologna is also famous for its cooking, claimed to be a form of Art here, which bestows upon the town another funny nick-name: *"La Grassa"* (the fatty town). In fact, cooked pasta such as *"Lasagne al forno"*, *"Tortellino in brodo"* and *"Bolognese meat sauce"* cannot be missed in the

View of Maggiore Square and its stunning architectural beauties

Restaurants in town. Finally, Bologna is also called " *la Turrita*", which means packed with towers, because of its countless towers and porticos (36 km of porticos are reckoned to form the body of the town). The following are the embassies in Bologna: Austrian, Belgian, French, German, San Marino, Swiss, Maltese, Polish, Principality of Monaco (Monte-Carlo), Costa-Rica (South-America) and Seborga (South-Africa).

HISTORICAL BACKGROUND

BEGINNINGS:
Etruscan Civilisation

The original inhabitants of the area, who left behind them articles of rare beauty and richness of design, are thought to belong to the Bronze Age (1200 BC).
However, the great number of tombs and pots found throughout the region, are believed to represent a later period, known as the Iron Age.
It seems likely that people from Liguria and Umbria settled the area at a time in which iron was first extracted and became a very useful metal. During the 9th century

Following page: Etruscan Sepulchres in "Giardini Margherita" Park

BC, clay and wooden huts thought to belong to a new settlement called *"Villanovian Centre"*, situated at what seemed to be a prosperous area which covered the rivers Panaro and Santerno, *"Valli di Comacchio"* (Comacchio Valleys) and the first ridge of the Apennines.

So strong was Greek influence here, but yet the area engaged neighbours in trade and a new town, acknowledged by *"Princepes Etruriae"* (the Etrurian Prince), was founded. *Felsina,* which was the first name given to Bologna, became a capital town importing ceramics, bronze objects and developing the art of working different metals.

During this period the dead would be buried for life hereafter; in fact, luxurious funerary furnishings consisted of many objects such as rings, earrings, necklaces, as well as pots, wine cups and jugs. Although Felsina, was claimed to be well populated and had flourished as a trade centre, famous for its pottery and bronzes, little or nothing remains of it nowadays.

By the 6th BC century to the beginning of the 5th century BC, Celtic populations, who were organised in tribes, continuously poured into Italy, subduing the Etruscan population. Invaders among Celtic populations were the *Gaels,* who settled in Emilia Romagna and the blueprint for a tribal society was in place. As a result, Felsina fell into decline becoming nothing more than a modest agricultural village.

Etruscan Sepulchres, which are exhibited at the Civic Museum of Archaeology, have been unearthed thanks to excavations of well-known archaeologists.

ROMAN EMPIRE AND
BARBARIANS' RAIDS

The desire of the Romans to forge northwards to Felsina united the Celtic tribes in opposition; to their surprise, the Romans encountered fearsome opposition.

Although a Celtic leader, called Hannibal, rallied a great number of warriors against the *"Roman war machine"*, his effort was not enough; in the year 202 BC the Roman Empire attacked the area and Celts were eventually defeated. A new name was given to the town: *Bononia* and even though they set up a network of well-made roads such as the famous Via Emilia (Via Aemilia), connecting Piacenza to Rimini, the new town preserved its quadrilateral shape: from *"Porta Ravegnata"* (East) to *"via Marconi-piazza Minghetti"* (West); and from *"via Farini-Barberia"* (South) to *"via Rivareno"* (North). During that time, the two main streets were via Indipendenza and via D'Azeglio whereas the backstreets were via Ugo Bassi and via Rizzoli. Basically, it looked like a fortified area with a surface of 50 hectare. Then, Bononia was turned into a Roman colony, economy flourished again and in 89 AD it was officially recognized as a Roman *"Municipium"* and its inhabitants became Roman citizens. During the Roman rule in Bononia, the town adopted the Roman style of life. So-called "popular politics" characterised the period and Bononia's citizens were sympathetic towards Roman Emperors such as Anthony and Augustus.

In 53 AD by the time Nero was proclaimed Roman Emperor, a wildfire spread through Bononia, which was then rebuilt by dint of hard work. Nevertheless, Bononia was thought to be one of the most prosperous towns throughout Italy. Finally, an 18 Km aqueduct took twenty years to complete and was pierced, wrecked and repaired on several occasions, as more and more plundering and raiding took place by the Barbarians.

MIDDLE-AGES OR DARK-AGES

Empire and Pontificate

The decline of the Roman Empire clashed with the raids of Barbarians, whose attacks were sudden and savage; the collapse of the Empire to the Barbarians left Bologna and in particular all the towns of Northern Italy in a severe state of disorganisation and confusion. This is proved by a letter written by Saint Ambrose in 343, who visited the town and had reckoned a period of misery and desolation. In 410 however grave the situation was, Bononia and its citizens were eager to fight against Barbarians who surprisingly were forced to retreat.

Later, in 553 Justinian, King of The Byzantines succeeded in conquering the town; it is in this period that Christianity spread and a decade of justice and order was being brought back. This idyllic time ceased in 728 when Longobards invaded Bononia and another war broke out.

Hence, Liutprand, the Longobard king, after having obtained the approval of the Pope, proclaimed himself the rightful heir of the Byzantine Empire. He demanded that Byzantines swear an oath of loyalty to him. Nevertheless, Longobards were finally defeated by Charlemagne; at the end of extended warfare Charlemagne gave Bononia to the Church. As a result, Bononia was ruled by the Church of Ravenna, which was reckoned to be one of the most powerful towns of the North of Italy. Severe contrasts are believed to have been caused by dissension between the Church and the Italian Kingdom (Impero Italico), concerning the sovereignty over Bononia. Hostilities ceased in 898 when it was decided that the Italian Kingdom (Impero Italico) would undertake the dominion over the town. However, over the next eight centuries the sovereignty over Bononia was to be constantly redefined.

During the 11th century walls surrounding the city centre and consisting of 18 entrances *(Torresotti)* were built.

Torresotto in Via San Vitale

This the period in which the richest families entertained themselves with a weird competition: building towers.
In fact it is estimated that about 200 towers have been built throughout those years.
The most famous ones, which are considered as being the symbols of the town, are: *Asinelli* Tower (98 metres) and *Garisenda* Tower (41 metres).

THE COMMUNAL AGE

It is during the 11th century that Bologna gained favour with both the Church and the Italian Kingdom.
This being the case, in 1115 Bologna was declared an independent *"Commune"* (Municipality) by Emperor Henry V, and therefore the town was given the possibility to appoint a local Consul chosen by the citizens annualy.

The Communal Palace and the Notaries' Palace

The fact that Bologna wanted to extend its prosperity and influence to all Emilia-Romagna had resulted in grave conflicts with other towns such as Modena, Imola and Ferrara.

The creation of *University* or *Studium* (1088-1115) represented an important event which affected all European cultures and whose origins combined with the birth of the Roman Law Studies School in Europe.

In 1152 Frederick "Barbarossa", the new Emperor, is believed to have been the first man to take great pains to unite Imperial Authority and the Independence of the Communes of Italy.

In this regard, he received support from the so-called four *"Glossatori"* of Roman Law Studies: Bulgaro, Martino, Jacopo and Ugo.

The expression "Glossatori"comes from a law subject called "Glossa".

In 1158, party leaders, representatives of the Church and the Empire authority, although being widely divided on political issues, reached a compromise; this being the case,

The Podestà Palace

it was decided that a new authority, *"Podestà"*, would be appointed to rule the town.

After a comparatively peaceful interlude, no sooner had a new Podestà been elected than new conflicts arose between his authority, and Consuls and Magistrates, which represented popular classes.

Accursio's grave in the courtyard of St. Francis' Basilica

On the other hand, disagreements between Empire and Communes of the country persisted and in the north of Italy a so-called *"Lombard League"* was founded.

Only when Alexander III, having been lectured at Bologna University, was refused the appointment as new Pope by Frederick Barbarossa, did Bologna decide to join the Lombard League. More civil wars broke out between Bologna and the towns of Romagna and Tuscany; only after the epic Battle of Legnano and the Peace Treaty of Constance (1183) was the Commune's authority recognised once again throughout Italy.

Many new Palaces were built in the centre of each town, *"Palazzi Comunali"*, to emphasise the Authority of the Communes; the aim was to decentralize the administrative and political power to other places around the country.

This is claimed to have been the most passionate period of the Communal Age characterised by continuous struggles between popular classes and the ruling aristocracy and on the other hand between Church and Empire.

As Bologna kept on increasing its rights, it soon became a powerful town in Emilia-Romagna. It is reported that in 1208 a new network of navigable canals was built and in 1219 annual trade fairs had been introduced. As soon as King Frederick II, who succeeded Frederick Barbarossa, tried to reassert the Empire authority throughout Italy, Bologna joined a second Lombard League formed in the north of Italy. Imperial troops were then defeated by Bologna on May 1249 on a bridge at *"Fossalta sul Panaro"* and Vincent (Enzo), King Frederick II's son, was held captive. Countless attempts were made by Frederick II to release his son from prison but he always failed.

On Frederick II death, Bologna grew more powerful and cities in Romagna were ruled by a Podestà elected by the town. In 1256 the Communes released an act, *"Liber Paradisus"*, in which it was declared that nobles would be deprived of servants who consequently became free citizens and were given the possibility to pay taxes to the Commune.

In addition, the general political situation in Italy at the time forced Bologna into a further dispute between two famous

Neptune Square

families: Guelfs, who belonged to Geremei family, and Ghibellines, who belonged to Lambertazzi family. The outbreak of the intermittent Forty Days' war involved also relatives of the two families living in other cities; final victory was for Guelfs family and on June 2, 1274 a quarter of Bologna population (out of 50,000 inhabitants) sympathetic towards Ghibellins, was forced to leave their native town and had to find political refuge mainly in Faenza, Forlì and Ravenna. However, their allegiance to the Empire was improved thanks to a close relationship, which was being created with Rudolf I from Hapsburg.

In 1278, as soon as Rudolf I withdrew his troops from Romagna, Bologna was forced to submit to the Church which exercised great privileges until 1859.

Meanwhile Ghibellines, allowed to return back, were evicted again after a period of six months.

SEIGNIORY

During the XIV century a new form of local government was created: the so-called *"Seigniory"*.

Great staircase in the King Vincent Palace (Palazzo Re Enzo)

It is reckoned that in 1325 another revolt broke out. This time the fight was between Bologna and Modena. As well as being defeated Bologna had to give in to the authority of the Cardinal Bertrando del Poggetto for about ten years. As a result, Taddeo Pepoli, appointed *"Captain of the people"* had managed to deprive the Church of her age-old power creating the first *"Seigniory"*. Taddeo died in 1347 and his two sons, whose names were Giovanni and Giacomo, were not as capable as their brave father so that Bologna was eventually sold to the very powerful Bishop of Milan: Giovanni Visconti. On Giovanni Visconti's death Bologna was first ruled by Giovanni da Oleggio in 1354 and then returned to the Pope in 1360, thanks to Aegidius from Alborraz, who conquered the town in 1361 (Battle of San Ruffillo) and swore an oath of loyalty to the Church. Despite Bologna being ruled by the Church, the city and its citizens desperately claimed freedom and independence. In this regard, more than one attempt is recalled: in 1376 an independent Republic was formed and in 1394 Giovanni I Bentivoglio, who belonged to a well-known family in Bologna tried to hold the power but he failed.

In 1398 it was the turn of Carlo Zambeccari and in 1401 Giovanni I Bentivoglio attempted a second time. He was then elected "Lord of Bologna" hoping to solve the problem; but unfortunately he was brutally murdered by Gian Galeazzo Visconti (Battle of Casalecchio). After a few months, Gian Galeazzo died and Bologna was once again the property of the Church.

During the XV century revolts and protests continued; consequently, in 1445 Annibale Bentivoglio managed to take control over the town but he was then killed. Later, Sante Bentivoglio, who succeeded Annibale Bentivoglio, ruled Bologna from 1462 to 1507. In peacetime this is reported to have been a period of great development especially in the arts and science field. The University grew more ambitious since education was notably encouraged and new buildings, monuments and Churches were erected as well.

However, once Cesare Borgia, named *"Il Valentino"*, came to power by means of violence he promptly returned Bologna to the Church which was anxious to re-establish power, on November 2 , 1506 (Pope Julius II). Giovanni Bentivoglio was forced to leave Bologna and in spite of attempts of the family Bentivoglio, the Church became more and more powerful.

DECLINE AND REFORM AGE

The new century brought to Bologna a period of complete anonymity. It has also to be emphasised that it was a time in which people would *"look into things since appearances were deceptive"*, as a famous politician of the time, Guicciardini, stated.

Even though Bologna was not considered a capital town anylonger, important events are claimed to have happened in the town; in fact, in 1515 Pope Leon X and Francis I met; in 1530 Charles V was proclaimed King of Italy and Emperor in the famous St. Petronius Church (Chiesa di San Petronio); additionally, in 1547 the *"Trent Council"* was transferred to Bologna.

However rich the social life in the town was, the ancient prestige of the University unfortunately declined. Being the case, the number of students decreased dramatically; only a little more than a thousand remained at Bologna University.

Neither was the economy improving; textile industry, trade, commerce and agriculture were affected by severe crises due to the growing competition, antiquated technology and low production.

But on the other hand, the School of Art, supported by influential painters such as Carracci, Guido Reni,

Dominichino and Guercino, continued to be prosperous.

During the XVI century a new institution was created: *"Saint Gregory Congregation"*, in which the poorer classes were being taken care of to harmonise criminality and diseases.

In 1593, Saturday was chosen as the *"merchant day"* and *"Piazza Maggiore"* (Maggiore Square) had then been indicated as the main site.

The purpose was to bring order and organisation. At that time, Bologna had been ruled by two Bishops from Boncompagni family for about half century.

No sooner had the English Revolution broken out and the new theories, which were being developed in France, had reached Italy, than Bologna responded to what can be defined an *"improving attitude"*; as new interest towards science spread all over the country and an Institute of Science was founded in Bologna by Luigi Ferdinando Marsili; the institute included new schools, museums, scientific materials and well educated teachers as well.

By the first decade of the XVIII century Bologna's population had reached 65,000; partly because life expectation

Beautiful Palace in via de' Toschi

was short, partly due to economic difficulties and being deprived of almost all their possessions, the number of aristocrats reduced to just a few hundreds.

Conversely, a war between Rome and Bologna broke out, and neither Cardinal Casoni nor Cardinal Origo were able to rectify the situation. Yet, when Prospero Lambertini, who later on became Pope Benedict XIV, was elected Cardinal of Bologna a new era started. Bologna's economy began to climb out of the doldrums, the University was equipped with new libraries and acquired its old importance once again. A study centre was opened and constantly supported by famous intellectuals of the period such as Aldrovandi, Marcello Malpighi, Luigi Galvani (famous for his studies on electricity), and Giovan Battista Martini.

In addition, a School of Journalism was founded and its most important representative was Ristori, famous for his *"Memorie Enciclopediche"*.

In 1740 the new Cardinal of Bologna, Aldrovandi, having won the confidence of the inhabitants, continued to support *"the improving attitude"* of the period.

In this regard, for fear of the revolutionary spirit of the French Revolution being widely accepted by Italians, the Church did her best to satisfy people's needs.

NAPOLEON AND RESTORATION

The Church's fears turned out to be sensible indeed! In fact, in 1794 the plot against the Pope, organised by people who were being influenced by the French Revolution, did not shake the Church whatsoever. The conspiracy was arranged by Luigi Zamboni, his father and De Rolando. Yet, little did their effort count since they all were convicted and executed.

Luigi Galvani's statue;
he was the first man to conduct studies on electricity

Napoleon and French troops arrived in Bologna on June 1796; it did not take too long for Napoleon, reckoned to be a man of insight, to gain favour with the town. In fact, he demanded that Bologna swear an oath of loyalty to the French Republic, a Bolognese minister, Antonio Aldini, was appointed to rule the town; therefore Bologna was left independent. Additionally, Napoleon approved of the creation of small Republic States based on the French models. Then, the *"Republic of Cispadania "* was founded and included: Reggio Emilia, Modena, Ferrara, Bologna and Romagna.

In 1799 Bologna was occupied by Austrian troops, and Bologna's luck seemingly run out. Bologna's inhabitants hoped that the French troops would come back; and that was the case; in 1800 French troops arrived in Bologna again; not only did they defeat the Austrians but they were also given *"the red carpet treatment"* by Bolognese people.

In spite of economic difficulties this was reckoned to have been a period of relative peace in which the idea of an *"Italian Republic"* was being discussed in Lyon by a group of Italians.

Nevertheless, after Napoleon had been defeated in Russia, Austrian troops conquered Bologna and allowed the Church to re-establish her power, according to the terms of the Congress of Vienna (1815).

ITALIAN RISORGIMENTO

The Church, being unable to cope with the present situation, tried hard to suppress rebellions with every means; however, as so often before, riots broke out in Bologna and elsewhere. People gathered together creating the so-called *"Sette"*, (1831), secret movements which were first started in Modena, thanks to Ciro Menotti, and soon spread all over the country.

Statue portraying Gregory XIII,
work of A. Menganti in the entrance gate of the Municipal Palace

In Bologna the aim of this movement was to give power to representatives of the middle-class such as professor Orioli and the solicitors Vicini, Zanolini and Silvani.

This bid for power set alarm bells ringing among the Austrians, who attacked Bologna and, by means of violence, established the Church's dominance over the town once again.

In 1842 Berti Pichat founded a newspaper, *"Il Felsineo"*, in which the innovative French economic and political systems were being analysed. Another newspaper *"Il Primato"* was started by Gioberti in which the idea of uniformity between Church and Government was being taken into account.

Another revolt was organised by rebels, who could not ignore the challenge in 1843; nevertheless it turned out to be a complete fiasco.

A new period, which was going to lead to the Constitution of 1848, had started. Bolognese revolutionaries allied themselves with the Italian King, Charles Albert, to face Austrians in Lombardy; unfortunately Charles Albert was defeated; as a result rebels Captain Giovanni Livraghi and Ugo Bassi faced capture and execution.

A second armed conflict soon followed in Bologna on 8 August 1848: popular classes gathered together and attacked the Austrian General, Welden, forcing the Austrians to leave the town; meanwhile Pope Pius IX pleaded with France to reassert her authority over Italy. Ten years of dreadful fights followed; Piedmont, which is a region in the north of Italy, grew stronger thanks to the abilities of a great leader, Cavour, who had always supported the revolutionary spirit of the time. Piedmont soon became an important State throughout all Europe.

Following page:
Monument commemorating the battle on August 8, 1848
Characteristic narrow alley in the city centre

On April 25, 1859 Italians, led by Victor Emmanuel and Austrians, fought another war; the conflict ended with victory for the Italians who had defeated the Austrian troops in the famous Battle of Magenta. Since the power of the Pope drew to an end, Bologna was finally declared an independent town and became part of Italian Kingdom (18 March 1860).

FROM ITALIAN KINGDOM
TO PRESENT TIME

Bologna, like most of the towns in Europe, became industrialised and urbanised. It was a process which dragged profound social, cultural and demographic change. Yet, lots of problems characterised the first decade of this period. Political debates and hostilities arose because of the inability to deal with economic and industrial issues. Various reforms were discussed with the aim of making economy more profitable. In 1871 the first working class movement, *"Fascio Operaio"*, was born and soon spread throughout Romagna.

It was on democratic basis that people wanted to launch the national industry and agriculture.

During this period an anti-Catholic newspaper, *"Il Resto del Carlino"* (1885), was printed, whose beliefs obviously contrasted with catholic newspapers such as *"Gazzetta dell'Emilia"*, *"La Patria"*, and *"Unione"*.

As political elections of 1913 brought the left wing party to power (Voto Rosso), Bologna was for the first time ruled by the new political class. At the end of the First World War thousands of people were left unemployed and homeless with Central Governments not being able to find any adequate solutions. However, in 1920, the

View of the Tower Clock from via D'Azeglio,
which is one of the most elegant street in town and famous for its lovely shops

left-wing party won political elections again. The gap between the right (Fascism) and the left parties became more and more marked. Being widely divided on political issues, violent revolts broke out; Fascism grew powerful; on November 1920 fascists attacked the Communal Palace in Bologna drawing to the end of the Socialist power in the town. In addition to which counsellor Giulio Giordani was killed.

Opponents were forced to leave Bologna and sought refuge elsewhere. Nevertheless, on October 31 1926 an attempt on Mussolini's life while visiting Bologna, was made by a fifteen-year-old boy, Anteo Zamboni, in Via Indipendenza. The youngster failed and was convicted and lynched on the spot.

But there is no doubt that during 1930s Fascism worked major improvements on the town life and on the economic field. A new railway, *"La Direttisima"*, connecting Bologna to Florence and to the very north of Italy (Brennero) was built and industry and transport recovered as well; at the beginning of the war Bologna had 322,000 inhabitants, a number that decreased dramatically as the war went on.

In 1941 conditions were appalling; many people died from starvation, diseases and poverty. On July 1943 Bologna was devastated by bombs twice and a huge number of people were killed; it was a fearsome raid which shocked the town.

During the same year Fascism sunk into decline and the Nazis occupation of the country began; people promptly responded to the attack by gathering to form the *"Partisan Party"* and therefore fight Nazism.

Bologna, which in November 1944 joined the CLN (National Liberation Committee), fought as well to overcome the enemy oppression. On April 21, 1945 the town was eventually liberated; on March 24, 1946 Giuseppe Dozza was elected Mayor of Bologna and his political power lasted for twenty years.

Reproduction of the Cistern, work of Francesco Terribilia placed in the second courtyard of the Communal Palace

URBANIZATION
OF THE TOWN

Observing the town's map it possible to find the location of its centre at first glance. During the Roman Empire period the town was located in the centre and the main streets were represented by both Via Indipendenza and Via D'Azeglio, whereas the backstreets by Via Ugo Bassi and Via Rizzoli.

The old *Forum* was placed in the point where *"cardo"* and *"decumano"* (two Roman architectural expressions) would meet. It still symbolises the heart of the town and forms Piazza Maggiore (Maggiore Square).

The old walls which once surrounded Bologna would expand in three directions: north, south and east. A Necropolis was built outside the walls and though it does not exist anylonger, it appears that human remains of

Ancient towers: Right, Dell'Arengo tower, Azzoguidi tower (Altabella). Centre, Prendiparte tower (Coronata). Left, the bell-tower of St. Peter's Cathedral

Saints Vitalis, Agricola and Petronius were kept there for a long time. Nowadays the monumental complex of St. Stephen (Santo Stefano) replaces the old Necropolis. It was during the 10th and 11th centuries that Bologna witnessed a rapid increase in the number of the population. In addition, many towers were built among which the most famous is *"Asinelli"* tower (98 metres).

During a war, fought in the 12th century against Emperor Frederick Barbarossa , additional walls (*Torresotti*) to surround Bologna were built in order to defend the town.

In 1220 Piazza VIII Agosto (VIII Agosto Square), was designed and chosen as the area on which to buy and sell cattle.

Bologna soon became a "gateway to war"; this being the case, in 1347 further walls to defend Bologna from severe attacks were constructed.

Porta Saragozza, one of the few which remains untouched

View of Porta Galliera from the stairs of Piazza XX Settembre
(XX Settembre Square)

This new barrier featured twelve so-called "Porte" (entrances), nine of which still exist: *San Vitale, Maggiore, Castiglione, Saragozza, San Felice, Lame, Galliera, Mascarella* and finally *San Donato*.
People began to build the characteristic "*Portici*" (porticos) partly because the town was often devastated by wars and fights, so that being not able to live outside the walls, they would rather expand their houses, and partly because porticos would protect them from rain, snow and sun. Originally, all porticos were made of wood which later on had been replaced with brick.
Palazzo Isolani (Isolani Palace) and *Palazzo Grassi* (Grassi Palace) are typical existing examples of buildings that underwent enlargement.

STUDIUM AND UNIVERSITY

No misgivings are given about the birthplace of University in Europe: Bologna.

This is one of the typical porticos of Bologna which have a total length of 36 Km

The famous wood and brick portico of Isolani Palace in Maggiore Square, claimed to be one of the first ever built in town.

Characteristic portico of Grassi Palace in via Marsala

The Studium was first founded in 1088; it is reckoned that at the end of the 1st century AD, Martial, reputed to have been a great Latin poet, emphasised Bologna as being "the erudite town" *(Culta Bononia)*. Additionally, the Byzantine Emperor Theodore II suggested that Bologna should be the place in which the Roman Law would be read (450 AD).

During the Dark-Ages or Middle-Ages, Sudium was the name given to a complex of schools, whilst University indicated group of people, both students and lecturers, who entered the building. From 1050 on, the Studium is claimed to have been the most famous place for *Roman Law Studies*. This being the case, Emperor Frederick Barbarossa showed great admiration for the solicitors graduated at Bologna (Dieta di Roncaglia 1158). Admiration was to reach the so-called *"Glossatori"* whose expression comes from a law subject called "Glossa". The most famous representatives "Glossatori" of the time were Irnerio, Accursio and the "Quattuor Doctores": Bulgaro, Martino, Jacopo and Ugo. Not only was Bologna appreciated for Roman Law Studies but also for the studying of other subjects such as *Theology* and *Rhetoric*, whose most well-known representative was Guido Guinizzelli, claimed to have been Dante's lecturer.

In 1140 a reform that separated Canon Law from Theology was carried out by monk Graziano Da Ghisi *(Decretum)*. In 1200 a great number of doctors were attracted to Bologna and in 1214 Ugo Borgognoni reached an agreement with the "Commune" that enabled him to exercise his profession in the town. Later on, in 1288, another Doctor, Taddeo Alderotti, was given the same privilege. It is reckoned that it was during this period that Doctor Modino De Liuzzi carried out important scientific studies about the human body.

In 1364 A College for Spanish students was founded (Collegio di Spagna). Further Colleges for students from other countries were built later. Nevertheless, it has to be emphasised in fact that due to political events and countless wars the Studium had often been subjected to severe economic difficulties.

In 1562 schools which formed the Studium such as St. Francis Church (Chiesa di San Francesco), St. Mary Dei Servi Church, (Chiesa di Santa Maria Dei Servi), St. Dominic Church (Chiesa di San Domenico) and others, were first transferred to "*Palazzo dell'Archiginnasio*" (Archiginnasio Palace) and then to "*Palazzo Poggi*" (Poggi Palace), in 1803. Poggi Palace and the Science Institute were later united to form what can be defined as the present University.

Many Italian writers and intellectuals attended Bologna University, such as Dante Alighieri (1285-1287); he mentions places and persons met in the town in "The Divine Comedy"; Francesco Petrarca (1323-1326), Nicolò Copernico (1496-1500), Torquato Tasso and others. Among the lecturers it is important to recall the two poets Giosuè Carducci (1860-1905) and Giovanni Pascoli; the surgeon Francesco Rizzoli, the physicist Augusto Righi and doctor Augusto Murri.

The year 1988 was the centenary of Bologna University's birth, which nowadays consists of thirteen faculties: Economics, Law Studies, Pharmacology, Chemistry, Agriculture, Engineering, Humanities Studies, Medicine and Surgery, Veterinary, Mathematics, Physics, Statistics, Demography and Politics.

TOURIST PROGRAMME 1

PIAZZA MAGGIORE (Maggiore Square)

Piazza Maggiore represents the heart of the town; its ancient buildings and glorious history make the square one of the greatest throughout Italy. It features a length of 115 metres and a width of 60 metres.

Originally, not only was the square the site in which merchandise was sold and bought, but also an area that witnessed great public celebrations and competitions between knights.

Glimpse of Maggiore Square from the Communal Palace

PALAZZO COMUNALE
(COMMUNAL PALACE)   west of Piazza Maggiore

The construction of this imposing building was carried out throughout several years by uniting different buildings. The clock tower, *"Torre dell'Orologio"*, was built in 1444 even though a real clock had been brought in later by Rinaldo Gandolfi in 1773. The well-known jurist, Accursio, used to live close to the clock tower in a house which was later acquired by the Commune of Bologna (1287). Part of the Palace was built at the end of 1500 for the use of Cardinal Legato, Governor of the town. At the top of the main portal is placed Pope Gregory XIII bronze statue, carved by Alessandro Sermenghi. Pope Gregory XIII is claimed to have reformed the calendar.

The building looks like a castle whose walls' construction began early in 1336. On the facade there is the "terracotta" (earthenware) made work *"Madonna col bambino"* (Virgin and child) carved by Nicolò dell'Arca in 1478. This work of Art depicts the Virgin showing her child.

View of the Communal Palace from Maggiore Square

La Fontana Vecchia, work of Tommaso Laureati (1505)

The part of the Palace that overlooks "Piazza del Nettuno" (Neptune Square) is covered with tablets in memory of those who died while defending the town. Farther along, great windows form a shrine in memory of the partisans who strove for the liberation of Bologna, between 1943-1945, *(Sacrario dei Caduti Partigiani)*. The shrine contains more than two thousand pictures. Inside the building there are two lovely courtyards; the first one, called "*Cortile d'Onore*" (the courtyard for the guests of honour), because famous people, while visiting Bologna, would stop there, is surrounded by lovely porticos. Conversely, in the second courtyard is placed the duplicate of the work of Art "La Cisterna" (The Cistern) by Francesco Terribila (1568). The original had been moved to the National Picture Gallery (Pinanoteca Nazionale). It is claimed that throwing a coin in the cistern will bring good luck.

Finally, the part of the building that overlooks via Ugo Bassi, is under construction and may be used as a Museum; close to this part of the Palace there is a beautiful fountain "*Fontana Vecchia*", work of Tommaso Laureati (1565).

Madonna and child on the facade of the Communal Palace, work of Nicolò dell'Arca

The long three naves of St. Petronius' Basilica

BASILICA DI SAN PETRONIO
(ST PETRONIUS BASILICA) south of Piazza Maggiore

The huge Basilica was built to honour Petronius, bishop of the town; it is reckoned to be one of the greatest Catholic churches throughout Italy and features a length of 132 metres, a width of 60 metres, a facade of 51 metres and finally a central vault of 41 metres.

St. Petronius' Basilica located in Maggiore Square

The three naves Basilica was designed by architect Antonio Di Vincenzo, in June 1390. This is the period in which the Commune was fighting against the Roman Church and willing to prove the independence of Bologna by any means. This being the case, as the Commune raised the money the works to build the biggest Church of Italy had begun. Unfortunately the designed construction was never completed because of the great disapproval of the Roman Church, who wanted to rule out the possibility of having a greater Church than St. Peters' in Rome. The facade, which was left incomplete as well, features eight saint busts in its marvellous marble base: *St. Florianus, St. Paul, St. Dominic, St. Augustine, St. Peter, St. Francis, St. Ambrose* and finally, *St. Petronius*.

The main portal was built under the direction of Jacopo della Quercia, in 1426; eleven chapels preserve the works of Art of the best Masters of the period such as Giovanni da Modena and his frescos called "*Storie dei Re Magi, Il Paradiso e L'Inferno*", kept in *Bolognina chapel (Cappella Bolognina);* Amico Aspertini and his work "*La Pietà e i Santi*", kept in the chapel of the Peace (*Cappella della Pace*).

Other features well worth mentioning include a sundial designed by G.D. Cassini and D. Guglielmini; the light comes in the building through a small hole located on the left aisle vault.

It appears that many celebrations occurred in the Basilica such as the coronation of Charles V, on February 24, 1530; as well, human remains of Elisa Bonaparte, Napoleon's sister, are still kept there.

A wooden miniature of the original project is preserved in the Church's museum.

*Aside: Detail of Giovanni da Modena's Fresco depicting "Hell",
inside the Basilica*

PALAZZO DEI NOTAI
(NOTARIES' PALACE) beside St. Petronius Basilica

A Notaries Association is believed to have been created in 1381 (*Socieà dei Notai*). In 1437 Fieravanti built the front side of the elegant Palace, whereas the six superb windows enriched with small marble pillars, had been carved by Antonio Di Vincenzo in 1385.

The Palace acquires a stylish and compact aspect and in the centre of the facade it is possible to notice a coat of arms of the Notaries Association, representing three ink bottles with goose-quills.

Notaries' Palace, elegant residence of the Notaries' Association

PALAZZO DEI BANCHI
(BANCHI PALACE)   in front of Palazzo Comunale
(Communal Palace)

While monetary exchanges were being done in the eastern part of the Square, the buildings in that area used to belong

View of Bianchi Palace from Maggiore Square

to powerful bankers (15th and the 16th centuries). Nowadays those buildings are elegant and sophisticated shops. Even though the construction first started in 1412 it was only later, in 1568, that they had been finished by dint of hard work of architect Jacopo Barozzi, whose nick-name was "*Il Vignola*". He built the Palace's facade and the portico which is part of the so-called "Portico del Pavaglione".

Behind the Palace it is possible to glimpse the magnificent dome of Chiesa di Santa Maria della Vita (St. Mary 's Life Church)

PORTICO DEL PAVAGLIONE
PALAZZO DELL'ARCHIGINNASIO
(PAVAGLIONE PORTICO AND ARCHIGINNASIO PALACE)

The name "*Pavaglione*" comes from a dialect word (*Pavaglio*) with which people would refer to the lucrative cocoon markets of the time, located in Piazza Galvani (Galvani Square). The Portico proceeds through Palazzo dei Banchi, the Civic Museum (Museo Civico), which originally was a Hospital (Ospedale di Santa Maria della Morte) and the Archiginnasio Palace (Palazzo dell'Archiginnasio).

The Archiginnasio Palace (Palazzo dell'Archiginnasio) was built under the direction of architect Antonio Morandi, called "*il Terribilia*", who set up the building in a record time of two years (1562-1564). It has to be emphasised in fact that the Pope himself firmly pressed ahead with the project on the grounds that it would stop the "Commune" from building the huge St. Petronius Basilica. Inside the Palace, which once was the seat of the Studium (University), is an impressive courtyard featuring more than 7,000 coats of arms used as emblems by noble families, scholars, chancellors and other well-known persons who

Theatre of Anatomy, located on the first floor of the Archiginnasio Palace

attended the Studium during the 16th and 17th centuries. On the first floor of the Palace, there is a *Theatre of Anatomy* in which anatomy classes were held; it is a carved room in which the teacher's desk features a rare canopy supported by two statues carved by Ercole Lelli. The statues depict two men without skin, "*Gli Spellati*". Very impressive as well, are two Lecture halls: "*Aula Magna degli Artisti*" (the Artists' Lecture-Hall) *and* "*Aula dei Legisti*" (the Jurists' Lecture-Hall). The second one was later named "*Stabat Mater*", from the famous opera written by Gioachino Rossini. These days, the Archiginnasio Palace is reckoned to be one of the most famous Italian municipal libraries because of its incredible number of volumes, more than 700,000 are claimed to be kept there, prints and epistles written by famous representatives of society. The refined material is accurately preserved and in perfect order thanks to Luigi Frati, who supervised the Archiginnasio Palace from 1858 to 1902.

PALAZZO DEI PODESTA'
(PODESTA' PALACE)   In front of St. Petronius Basilica

The Palace was built in 1200 for the politicians of the time who would meet in there to take important decisions. However, the building turned out to be far too small and therefore had been enlarged in 1245. The new Palace, "*Palatium Novum*" was later renamed Palazzo Re Enzo (King Vincent Palace). The Palace features two courts from which a vault takes shape; in each corner of the vault were carved four earthenware statues depicting "I Patroni della città" (Patrons of the town) by Alfonso Lombardi (1525). A peculiar feature of the Palace is the fact that when two persons whisper to each other from opposite corners of the vault, it is possible to hear the voices quite clearly.

The Podestà Palace located in Maggiore Square

A tower, "*Torre dell'Arengo*" was built in 1212 at the top of the vault; in the event of the bell being rung, its sound would inform people of either military or political events. The expression "*Arengo*" originated from the word "ringhiera", a handrail surrounding the front part of the tower from which not only were ordinances or sentences read out but also criminals would be hanged. In 1484 Giovanni II Bentivoglio wanted the Palace to be restored but yet the restoration had never been carried out. On the upper floor of the building there is a huge and unique Hall entirely painted between 1911 and 1928 by Alfonso De Carolis and some of his scholars.

Neptune Square by night

PALAZZO DEL NETTUNO
(NEPTUNE PALACE)

The Palace was officially opened in 1564; it is located between "Palazzo Comunale" (Communal Palace) and "Palazzo Re Enzo" (King Vincent Palace) and connected to "Piazza Maggiore" (Maggiore Square). Well worth mentioning is one of the most famous works of Art of Bologna: "la Fontana del Nettuno" (Neptune Fountain), which was built in the square's centre.

FONTANA DEL NETTUNO
(NEPTUNE FOUNTAIN)

In the centre of Neptune Square

The fountain was built by a great Flemish sculptor, Jean Boulogne De Donai called "il Giambologna", mainly to plans originally drawn up by architect Laureati. It represents *Neptune* cooling down water; people from Bologna usually refer to Neptune Fountain as "*il gigante*" (the giant); in fact it is 3.20 metres tall and weights 22 quintals. Not only does the marble base of the fountain depict a Papal coat of arm but also mythical creatures such as sirens, dolphins and others creatures , are exquisitely represented. The old railing which once surrounded the fountain had been removed in order to give tourists the possibility to grasp every single detail of this gorgeous work of Art.

Detail of one of the four small fountains which remains untouched, at the main fountain's top

The Neptune Fountain, work of Gianbologna (1563)

PALAZZO RE ENZO   east of Neptune Square
(KING VINCENT PALACE)

Since "Palazzo dei Podestà" (Podestà Palace) turned out to be far too small to hold the great number of politicians of the time, the building was enlarged in 1245 and called "*Palatium Novum*". The Palace was later called King Vincent Palace, as Vincent, King of Sardinia, had been held prisoner in the Palace for twenty-three years.

Originally the ground floor was used as a weapons' warehouse and a "Carroccio", a sort of four wheels car equipped with altar, bell, and flags symbolising freedom, was carefully stored up for "any appropriate occasion". Two lovely Halls, "*Il salone dei Trecento*" and "*Il Salone dei Podestà*" and a beautiful staircase winding up from the Court contribute to the splendour of the Palace. The latest restoration was made in 1905 by architect Alfonso Rubbiani.

View of King Vincent Palace from via Rizzoli

TOURIST PROGRAMME 2

Should you be in Via Clavature, a side street leading off from "Portico del Pavaglione " (Pavaglione Portico), please do not miss out **"Santa Maria della Vita"** Church, designed in 1289 as a Hospital in which the disabled were cared for. In 1687 the building was changed into a Church and the huge copper dome, built by Giuseppe Tubertini, was added in 1787. Most of the freestanding sculptures were executed by Nicolò dell'Arca, *"Compianto sul Cristo morto"* (1485-1490) and Alfonso Lombardi, *"I Funerali della Vergine"* (1522).

At the bottom of this narrow street you could turn right and gaze at a construction which at first glance might

Church: Santa Maria della Vita, in via Clavature

Church: Santa Maria della Vita;
earthenware masterpiece of Nicolò dell'Arca

remind of a castle. Nevertheless, it is a complex of buildings that form "**Palazzo Pepoli**" (Pepoli Palace).

Its facade is bent to suit the flow of River Aposa, which is nowadays under the ground.

The ceilings of the building were painted by the most famous artists of the 17th century such as Crespi, Creti and others. Carrying on towards "le due Torri" (the two famous towers), you will meet "**Piazza della Mercanzia**" (Merchandise Square) and a few medieval buildings such as "**Palazzo della Mercanzia**" (Merchandise Palace), built in 1382 under the direction of architect Antonio di Vincenzo. Originally the Palace, residence of an "Arts' Association", was used as a *Merchants' Forum* to discuss disputes between purchasers and customers.

Square Mercanzia: Bolognini Palace and Seracchioli House

The Beautiful facade of the Merchandise Palace, located in Mercanzia Square

The facade features a marble balcony with a great canopy made by brothers Dalle Masegne; a combination of a group of sculptures, depicting *Justice St. Peter and St. Petronius*, and the beautiful coat of arms belonging to the Arts' Association, make the balcony one of the nicest throughout Bologna's monuments.

From "Piazza della Mercanzia" it is possible to walk along Via Santo Stefano (St Stephen Street) and finally meet the splendid "**Basilica di Santo Stefano**" (St. Stephen Basilica), which is formed by seven Churches different in style, colour and shape.

This group of Churches is thought to be the most ancient monument in Bologna and St. Petronius himself, bishop and protector of the town, is indicated as having designed the Basilica in 983. The project was called "*Santa Hierusalem*", from Latin, because of similarities to the Holy Sepulchre in Jerusalem. During the 11th-century "*Chiesa del Crocefisso*" (the Holy Cross Church), a cellar and a presbytery belonging to the Basilica had always been considered as two separated Churches.

Facade of St. Stephen's Basilica

St. Stephen's Basilica:
Saint Sepulchre Church in which St. Petronius' grave is preserved

St. Petronius' tomb *(431-450)* is preserved in the so-called *"Chiesa del Santo Sepolcro"* (The Holy Sepulchre Church), which was built during the 5th century and later restored during the 12th century.

A lovely marble basin, in which believers would throw coins, is placed in the courtyard, "Cortile di Pilato", adjacent to the church.

The following Church is *"Chiesa della Trinità"*, famous for its heavy ornate crosses carefully placed in three niches and representing Christ and the two thieves.

Finally, human remains of Saints Vitalis and Agricola are kept in two sepulchres made of stone in the 5th century church *"Chiesa di San Vitale e Agricola"* (St.Vitalis and St. Agricola Church). In addition, a magnificent Roman cloister is located very close to the group of the seven Churches.

The beautiful St. Martin's crypt

St. Stephen's Basilica: Pilato's courtyard

*St. Stephen's Basilica:
Saints Vitalis and
Agricola Church*

61

Not far away from Piazza Santo Stefano (St. Stephen Square), is a little upward slope that leads to another beautiful Church, called "**San Giovanni in Monte**"; the Church was built during the 5th century and underwent restoration quite a few times between the 13th and the 15th centuries. The earthenware eagle, installed on the Church's facade, is work of Nicolò dell'Arca. The three long gothic naves were decorated by different artists throughout the centuries. Other works by Guercino, Lorenzo Costa are preserved in the chapels in which is also placed a duplicate of the famous "*Santa Cecilia*" (St. Cecily) by Raffaello, painted by Clemente Alberti; the original one is preserved in the National Picture Gallery. Eventually, beautiful cloisters were carved by Terrabilia in an old monastery close to the Church; the monastery, which had been a prison until 1986, is now being reconstructed and due to open as a Museum.

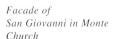

*Facade of
San Giovanni in Monte
Church*

TOURIST PROGRAMME 3

From Via Rizzoli (Rizzoli Street) you can reach "**Porta Ravegnana**", originally considered as an important road junction towards Ravenna (Via San Vitale), Rimini (Strada Maggiore that becomes Via Aemilia) and finally, Tuscany (Via Santo Stefano).

The small square gives birth to what are believed to be the emblems of the town, "**le due torri**" (two towers): **Asinelli** tower (98 metres) and **Garisenda** tower (48 metres). Both towers were built in the 12th century as a result of the competition between two Bolognese families. Unfortunately Garisenda's foundations were definitely not solidly supported and for fear of the tower collapsing people decided to reduce its length from 61 metres to a little more than 48 metres. As a consequence, family Asinelli won the competition.

Saints Bartholomew and Gaetano Church bell-tower and dome

Saints Bartholomew and Gaetano Church: external chapel, decorated by Edoardo Collamarini

The symbols of Bologna: Asinelli and Garisenda towers

The so-called "leaning tower" of Bologna struck Dante as being extremely impressive. This being the case, he mentions a similar tower in his work "The Divine Comedy".

Conversely, Asinelli tower is considered as a heavy one, in fact it weights 8,500 tons and features a quite low barycentre. In 1488, a military loggia, *"Rocchetta"*, was added to the tower, which in 1493 was struck by lightning but yet survived.

A gorgeous Palace, built in 1486 by Giovanni Piccinini, is located between Via Rizzoli and Porta Ravegnana. The Palace can be called by two different names: either *"Casa dei Drappieri"* or *"Casa degli Strazzaroli"*.

As soon as you reach Strada Maggiore you are bound to notice the "**Basilica di San Bartolomeo e Gaetano**" (St. Bartholomew and Gaetano Basilica), situated on the left side of the street. The Basilica and its beautiful portico had been built in 1516, whereas the stunning dome and bell were added later, in 1694. Lovely frescos adorn the interior of the Basilica, done by famous artists such as Francesco Albani, Guido Reni, *"Madonna con il figlio addormentato"*, and Ludovico Carracci, *"San Carlo addormentato"*; on the other hand, the ornate chapel is work of Edoardo Collamarini.

Walking along to your right you will meet the splendid "**Casa Isolani**" (Isolani House) and its suggestive wood and brick portico, built in 1250.

If you feel tired, hungry or eager to do some shopping you certainly happen to be in the right place! In fact, if you wish to rest your body and get more comfortable you can always pop in the so-called "Court", which leads straight to Piazza Santo Stefano (St. Stephen Square) and has lovely Italian restaurants, shops and bars.

Going back to Srada Maggiore, you should not miss one of the most appreciated Churches by Bolognese people and its peculiar square-portico: "**Santa Maria dei Servi**". On December 13 the Church celebrates Saint Lucy and a lovely Christmas market is placed outside the building. Built in 1346, the Church was enlarged and altered in 1386 under the

View of the Isolani Palace from St. Stephen's Square

The magnificent square portico in front of the Church named Chiesa dei Servi

direction of Andrea Manfredi; but it was only in 1500 the Church's construction was completed.

Not only will you appreciate a marble altar built by G.A. Montorsoli, but also a magnificent mechanical organ built by teacher Tamburi. One of the two chapels of the Church preserves the work of Art "*la Madonna col bambino*" painted by Cimabue, while works by Guido Reni (*Quattro Angeli*) and other artists are kept in the monastery.

The long square portico, which surrounds the Church, was started between 1393 and 1515 and completed in 1855.

"**Palazzo Davia Bargellini**" (Davia Bargellini Palace), designed in 1658 and built under the direction of Bartolomeo Provaglia, is believed to be one of the most important monuments of XVII century. Two huge statues, called "*I Telamoni*", carved by Brunelli and Agnesini, support the bal-

Facade of Davia Bargellini Palace, famous for its Museum

cony on the Palace's facade. Should you be interested in antiques you could visit the "*Davia Bargellini Museum*" inside the Palace, which preserves a lovely 18th-century puppet theatre.

Passing by "Piazza Aldrovandi" (Aldrovandi Square), which is the site of the "herbs market", you will see **"Palazzo Fantuzzi"** (Fantuzzi Palace). The Palace, built in 1520 by architect Andrea da Formigine, was the residence of rich merchants, who had been Senators of Bologna between 1467 and 1749. The interior of the Palace is the work of Trachini, who designed both the chapel and the great staircase; finally, two huge elephants, "*Elefanti*", carrying a castle on their backs, were carved on the Palace facade.

Once you are at the end of via San Vitale you can go back to piazza Porta Ravegnana.

Facade of Palace Fantuzzi, believed to be the work of Andrea da Formigine

TOURIST PROGRAMME 4

If you are walking along Via Rizzoli, direction two towers "Le due Torri", you can turn right (Via Zamboni) and reach both "Piazza Rossini" (Rossini Square) and "**San Giacomo Maggiore**" Church. The Church's construction started in 1267 as requested by the monastic order, "*Agostiniani*", and was completed in 1344. The roman-gothic style Church's facade features an impressive portal supported by two carved lions and *Saint Giacomo's* statue.

In 1445 Annibale Bentivoglio had bought a chapel as a present for his beloved family; the chapel, which was decorated by F. Francia, "*Madonna e i Santi*" and L.Costa, "*Portray of Giovanni II*", still preserves works by Ludovico Carracci (*Saint Rocco),* Pellegrino Tibaldi and his frescos in *Poggi chapel (Cappella Poggi)*, Innocenzo da Imola, Jacopo della Quercia, Paolo Veneziano and others.

At the bottom of the characteristic portico, you will find the "**Oratorio di Santa Cecilia**" (St. Cecily Oratory), a tiny Roman church which, thanks to the work of great artists such as Francia , Costa and Aspertini (1504), is considered important proof of Bolognese Art of the Restoration period.

Close to the Church, is the "*Conservatorio Musicale G.B. Martini*" (Academy of music). The Academy, which originally was a monastery, was built in 1804 and reckoned to have had scholars who were bound to be in the musical firmament such as Rossini and Donizetti. In addition, the Academy has also a *"Museo Civico Bibliografico Musicale"* (Bibliography Civic Museum on music works), in which is preserved one of the most complete classic music collections throughout Italy. "Piazza Rossini" (Rossini Square) shows two more Palaces: "**Palazzo Malavezzi**" (Malavezzi Palace), built by Jacopo Barozzi and restored by Andrea da Formigine and finally, **"Palazzo Salem"** (Salem Palace) in which is the fresco by of Carracci brothers, *"Storia della fondazione di Roma"* (History of Roman's foundation)

Facade of St. Giacomo Maggiore Church

Whether you are an "opera freak" or not you should visit the famous "**Teatro Comunale**", (Municipal Theatre) which is a five minute walk from "Piazza Rossini" to "Piazza Verdi". The theatre was designed by Antonio Bibiena and opened in 1763; the hall is divided into five different types of boxes and can hold 1,200 spectators. Reckoned to be the second most ancient theatre throughout Italy (the actual most ancient is "Teatro San Carlo" in Napoli), it had been brightened up throughout the years thanks to performance of great artists such as Wagner. Besides this, the theatre has been

St. Giacomo Maggiore
Church: detail of Ludovico
Carracci's "San Rocco"

Below:
the Communal Theatre
located in Verdi Square

Interior of the Communal Theatre

organizing the "International Jazz Festival" for fifteen years. Initially, the theatre was a Palace called "Palazzo dei Bentivogli" and had been knocked down as a consequence of a civil war, which broke out in 1507; the adjacent street to the theatre was named *"Via del Guasto"* (the street in which the damage had occurred) to commemorate the civil war.

Impossible not to stress the fact that Via Zamboni represents the heart of University whose Administration building is represented by **"Palazzo Poggi"** (Poggi Palace), built in 1549; the building features frescos by Tebaldi and Nicolò dell'Arca, as well as a tower, *"Torre della Specola"* (1712-1725). The different University's faculties are spread out in Via Zamboni, Via Irnerio and Porta San Donato.

The gothic **"Basilica di San Martino"** (St. Martin's Basilica), which was first built by the monastic order, *"Carmelitani Scalzi"*, is located in Via Marsala; due to political events and wars the Basilica had been rebuilt a few times between 1217

St. Martin's Basilica

and 1879 and the latest restoration was in 1929. Artists such as Ludovico Carracci, Francia, L.Costa, Girolamo da Carpi, B.Cesi and Amico Aspertini were responsible for a great deal of the frescos in the Church's chapel. Evidence of remains of the previous Church are shown in the "*16th-century cloister*" in which is also preserved a work of Art of Lucio Massari, "*San Tommaso Carmelitano*".

If you like walking in the lovely narrow streets of the city centre, provided that you possess a good map in order not to get lost, you could go to Via Altabella and visit the 13th-century "**Palazzo Arcivescovile**"; naturally, a portico will guide you directly to the Palace. Once you enter the Palace's courtyard you will be struck by two towers: "*Torre Altabella*" (61m) and "*Torre Prendiparte o Coronata*" (59m). The second tower is also called "the crowned tower" (Coronata) as the top looks like a crown and was used as a prison. Finally, from Via Altabella you may go back to the main Via Rizzoli.

TOURIST PROGRAMME 5

From "Piazza del Nettuno" (Neptune Square), you could easily take the grand Via Indipendenza; at the top of this pedestrian street on the right you can gaze at 10th-11th-century "**Cattedrale di San Pietro**" (St. Peter Cathedral), called "*metropilitana*" in 1582 by Pope Gregory XIII. Had it not been for a wildfire which spread out in 1131 and an earthquake in 1575 the old Cathedral would not have been rebuilt so many times. Having pointed out that, the Cathedral was later restored by Floriano Ambrosini and Alfonso Torreggiani between 1600 and 1605. The huge statues representing *St. Peter and St. Paul* dominating the Church's facade were carved by Agostini Corsini and P.A. Verschaffelt, while Torregiani designed the splendid central aisle inside the Cathedral. The Roman presbytery features the last work of Ludovico Carracci, "*Annunziata*" (1486), while eight earthenware statues shaped by Alfonso Lombardi in 1500 are placed in the crypt of the Church. Finally, a gorgeous Roman

St. Peter's Cathedral: right, statue portraying the Saint,
placed on the left corner of the facade

square bell-tower dominates the entire building. The 15th-century Church called"**Madonna di Galliera**" is located in a street close to Via Indipendenza, Via Manzoni; were it not for atmospheric pollution and climate conditions it would feature a great facade, designed in 1491. The Church used to belong to the monastic order called *"Filippini"* or *"Padri dell'Oratorio"* and adjacent to the Church you will see an ornate oratory, which was built by Alfonso Torreggiani.

Going back to Via Indipendenza you can have a look at a theatre called "**Teatro Arena del Sole**", which was built in 1810, mainly to plans originally drawn up by Carlo Asparri. Its facade shows statues carved by Alfredo Neri.

If you continue further Via Indipendenza you will meet an important square: "**Piazza VIII Agosto**", site of the great battle in which Austrians troops were defeated (8 August 1848). A monument, depicting a man running the flag on the Austrians' dead bodies, was built to commemorate "that day of freedom".

On the small hill dominating "Piazza VIII Agosto" there used

Facade of the theatre "Arena del sole"

to be a fortress, *"Fortezza di Galliera"*, which was later, in 1683, transformed into a Public Park; nowadays it is called *"Parco della Montagnola"* because of lovely open air-markets that lure a great number of Italians and foreigners every Friday and Saturday. A few fountains enrich the Park, among which the most attractive is the one placed at the bottom of a great staircase that leads to the square called "Piazza XX Settembre"; the fountain was built by T. Azzolini and A.Muggia, in 1983 and features well worth mentioning include a group of sculpture carved by Diego Sarti, representing a horse and a woman attacked by an octopus. Eventually, it is possible to admire two gorgeous Palaces located in Via Galliera: the elegant *"Palazzo Montanari"*, which has a great library, *"Palazzo Aldrovandi"* (1725), *"Palazzo Felcini"* and the XVII century Church *"Santa Maria della Pioggia"*, in which is preserved a work of Art of Agostino Carracci, *"Natività"*.

Sculptures carved below the staircase of Piazza XX Settembre

Staircase illuminated by street lamps

TOURIST PROGRAMME 6

Police headquarters *(Questura)* are located in "Piazza Galileo" (Galileo Square) whereas the residence of Bologna local authority *(Prefettura)* is in a Palace close to "Piazza Roosevelt". A Church called **"San Salvatore"**, was built in 1149 and restored in 1605, under the direction of Antonio Magenta; the Church is in a tiny square in Via Cesare Battisti. Quite interesting is the Church's library that once represented an important culture centre, especially for English students who would meet and study in the building. Beautiful paintings of Innocenzo da Imola, Cavedoni and Vitale, "*L'Incoronazione della Vergine Madonna* e *Madonna della Vittoria*" are preserved in the Church's chapels; in addition, the group of statues on the Church's facade representing "*I Quattro Evangelisti*" (Four Evangelists), were carved by Todeschini.

In front of San Salvatore Church, is "**Palazzo Marescalchi** (Marescalchi Palace). The building was the residence of Senators and shows one of the greatest halls in all Bologna, in which magnificent work of Arts of Guido Reni *"Aria e Fuoco"* (1612) and Ludovico Carracci *"Allegoria dell'onore"*, are accurately preserved.

When you reach "Piazza Malpighi" (Malpighi Square) you are bound to notice a copper statue depicting *"l'Immacolata"* (Virgin Mary), carved by Guido Reni in 1638; the statue had been placed at the top of a pillar in the square's centre.

Beside the statue it is impossible not to look at a noble example of Gothic architecture: the 13th-century "**Basilica di San Francesco**" (St. Francis Basilica)**,** founded by a great monastic order, the Grey Friars (Franciscans). It appears that during his visit in Bologna, St. Francis firmly expressed his beliefs on peace and faith; people and the local authority moved by the Saint's speeches, decided to build a Church to honour him (1235-1263). The majestic building is a three aisles Church and holds nine chapels. In 1798, according to Napoleon's wish, the Basilica was converted into a Customs and Excise House depriving it of its religious role. Only after having undergone renovation, in 1928, was the Church opened again. During the second world war the Basilica, which had been completely knocked down, was restored a second time thanks to the hard work of architect Alfredo Barbacci. The sepulchre of Alexander V, who died in Bologna in 1410, is placed in the left aisle while 14th century funeral monuments of University's Chancellors are preserved in the cloister called *"Chiostro dei Morti"*. Three more tombs of the famous "Glossatori" *Accursio, Odofredo and Rolandino,* are kept in the Church's garden; finally, the biggest bell-tower was built by Antonio Di Vincenzo. Walking along Via Nosadella you will come to Via Saragozza in which is located another beautiful Palace built in the first decade of the 16th-century: "**Palazzo Albergati**" (Albergati Palace) which used to belong to a rich and powerful family in Bologna

External part of St. Francis' Basilica and Glossatori's graves

Facade of St. Francis' Basilica

(Albergati family). Going back to the city-centre you will meet the ornate 14th-century **"Collegio di Spagna"** (Spanish College), residence of noble Spanish students. Decorations were made by Andrea da Formigine; the College features two courtyards: a 16th -century courtyard and a 14th century courtyard. The chapel, "Cappella di San Clemente", features

Facade of St. Paul's Church

frescos of Crespi, M. Zoppo and Andrea di Bartolo. Not far away from the Spanish College, is the one aisle "**Chiesa di San Paolo**" (St. Paul's Church), built in 1611 under the direction of architect Ambrogio Magenta. The Church used to belong to the monastic order of *Barnabiti*; a Roman style facade was added to the original building in 1636; the chapels preserve paintings by Ludovico Carracci and his "*Paradiso*" (Paradise) and Ludovico Carracci and his "*Purgatorio*" (Purgatory). Besides this, a group of sculptures, carved by Alessandro Algardi, are placed on the great altar. Eventually, an elegant 15th-century Church is located in Via Val d'Aposa:"**Chiesa dello Spirito Santo**". The Church used to belong to the monastic order of *Celestini*. Its facade features earthenware decorations and five huge medals portraying Jesus Christ, Mary, St. Benedict, St. Jhon and Pope St. Celestine.

Spirito Santo Church,
via Val d'Aposa

TOURIST PROGRAMME 7

In Via D'azeglio you will be wondering at the fantastic accuracy with which the creator worked the stone facade of the stylish **"Palazzo Bevilacqua"** (Bevilacqua Palace), built by Niccolò Sanuti in 1447; unfortunately the gorgeous facade is now being eaten up by climate conditions. A lovely tiny balcony, which features an iron handrail, was built on the main entrance of the building. A group of earthenware statues is placed in the Palace's courtyard whose centre is enriched with a pretty stone fountain, representing a lion supported by a pillar. In 1547 a group of prelats, participating to the *"Concilio Tridentino"*, held in the Palace, sheltered in the the town to escape from a terrible plague. In 1484 the Palace was sold to Giovanni II Bentivoglio and later to Cardinal Campeggi; finally, the building was sold to Senator Bevilacqua in 1793.

St. Proloco Church, **"Chiesa di San Proloco"**, stands in the

Facade of the Bevilacqua Palace, via D'Azeglio

lovely Via D'Azeglio; "Proloco" was the name of a brave soldier who converted to Christianity (303) and therefore had been persecuted by Diocletian; human remains of three "Glossatori" *Ugo , Bulgaro*, *Martino* and soldier *Proloco* are kept inside the Church. Other features well worth mentionig include a splendid *marble ark*, which hold human remains of the Saint, and the painting representing *San Benedict*, by Bartolomeo Cesi. Four cloisters, built by Terrabilia and Tibaldi, are placed in the old monastery, which nowadays is used as a Maternity Hospital.

In addition, a female monastery called, "**Chiesa Corpus Domini**" founded by *St. Caterina Dè Vigri*, was built in 1456; the Saint was born in Bologna in 1413 and her body and important manuscripts are still preserved in the ornate cellar, decorated by Franceschini; the latest restoration of the

Earthenware doorway of Corpus -Domini Church

monastry was in 1687.

Walking along Via Tovaglia you will come to the majestic "**Palazzo di Giustizia**" (Justice Palace), designed and constructed by Andrea Palladio in 1534; the Palace was sold in 1822 to Napoleon's brother-in-law, Prince Felice Baciocchi; features well worth mentioning include a beautiful courtyard and the great staircase inside the building, which was only later converted into the house of the Justice Courts.

During the 13th century the monastic order Black Friars (*Dominicans*) founded the **"Basilica di San Domenico"** (St. Dominic's Basilica), called "Santa Maria delle Vigne".

On St. Dominic's death (1221), with the passing of the centuries the old Church underwent several restoration; in fact, not only was the building enlarged but also new chapels had been added. The three aisles Church was finally restored by a quite famous Bolognese architect, Carlo Francesco Dotti,

Justice Palace (Palazzo di Giustizia or Palazzo Baciocchi

St. Dominic's Basilica, in front of St. Dominic's Square

in 1728.

The 15th-century masterpiece "*l'Arca marmorea di San Domenico*" (St. Dominic's marble Ark) is placed in the presbytery; the first version of the beautiful Ark (1267) was the work of Nicolò Pisano; in 1469 the Masterpiece had been enriched with a stunning marble cyma and statues portraying God, Saints and angels. This second version was carried out by another artist, Nicolò da Puglia or better "Nicolò dell'Arca" (Nicolò who built the Ark). Finally, *St. Petronius* and *St. Proloco* statues were carved by Michelangelo. The greatest marble chapel, which forms a huge dome, was built in 1597 by Floriano Ambrosini and features frescos by Guido Reni, "*Glorificazione del Santo*" (1613).

Other works of Art by Ludovico Carracci, Guido Reni, Cesi, Calvart *(I Misteri)*, as well as paintings by Guercino (*San Tommaso*), Carracci (*San Raimondo*) and Bartolomeo Cesi (*l'Adorazione dei Magi*), are kept in Rosario chapel.

In front of the Church two huge pillars depicting St. Dominic (1627) and *Madonna del Rosario* (1632) stand in

the square; between them is placed Rolandino De Passeggieri's tomb; he was the notary who wrote a letter to King Frederick II in which he was informed of the fact that his son ,Vincent, would be held prisoner in Bologna; eventually, the 18th-century portico was knocked down in 1909.

VARIOUS PROGRAMMES

CHIESA DELLA MADONNA DEL BARACCANO
MADONNA DEL BARACCANO CHURCH
(Piazza del Baraccano 2- Baraccano square)

The term *"Baraccano"* comes from the name of the towers that belonged to the old walls of the town. Originally, the Church, built in 1402, was a local charity,*"Confraternita di*

Preceding page: the marble Ark placed in St. Dominic's Basilica.
Above, Madonna del Baraccano Church

Ancient walls of Madonna del Baraccano Church

Santa Maria", to help people in need and provide medical facilities. A work of Art by Francesco Cossa (1472) portraying a *Madonna*, is kept in an ornate marble inside the Church. The nice Church's dome, built by Agostino Barrelli, was added only later in 1682.

Bologna's long tradition suggests that on their wedding day, the bride and the groom should go to the Church and pray for the Madonna to protect them and their marriage.

It doesn't always work, though!!!

A lovely Park, "**Giardini Margherita**", is just a five minutes walk from Madonna del Baraccano Church. The area was built in 1875 to celebrate the first Italian Queen whose name was Margherita. You can roam around Bologna's greatest Park which offers you nice surroundings or just take a rest beneath its trees and, who knows, you might even drift off to sleep for a while.........or, if you still want to pour your energy into cultural matters you can always have a look at the etruscan sepulchres placed all over the park or at the copper statue depicting King Victor Emmanuel II.

CHIESA DI SAN MICHELE IN BOSCO
ST. MICHELE IN BOSCO CHURCH
(Piazzale San Michele 5)

Originally the Church was given in 200 to a great monastic order, *Agostiniani*. After a terrible plague, which spread quickly killing large numbers of people, the Church had been transformed into a fortress and a chapel was built beside it. In 1430 a wildfire, due to wars between Bentivogli family and Canetoli family, had severely damaged the building; the Church underwent restoration beteween 1437 and the first decade of 1600. With the passing of the centuries, the building had been subjected to radical changes; in fact, it was used as a barracks in 1797, as a prison in 1804 and finally transformed into an existing Orthopaedic Hospital, in 1896. The Hospital, which was set up by doctor Francesco Rizzoli, had been named "*Istituto Ortopedico Rizzoli*" (Orthopaedic Institute Rizzoli) to honour its founder.

San Michele in Bosco Church, restored in 1494

The building is located on a 157 metres hill which dominates Bologna. Archangel Gabriel Church, *(Chiesa Arcangelo Gabriele)* is in the North part of the construction, and was restored in 1494 thanks to great artists such as Ludovico Carracci and Guido Reni. The central vault is work of B. Peruzzi whereas the beautiful facade, portico and bell-tower were designed and built by B. Rossetti in 1523.

Eventually, the exact measurement of the greatest buildings in Bologna are imprinted on the surface floor of a 162 metres lodge of the building.

SANTUARIO DELLA MADONNA DI SAN LUCA
SHRINE OF MADONNA DI SAN LUCA
(Via San Luca 36)

The shrine was built on rising hill, *"Colle della Guardia"*, that overlooks Bologna. Most believers venerate the Madonna painting, *"Beata Vergine"*, preserved in the shrine

Below and following page: Shrine of Madonna di San Luca

that, according to popular's beliefs, had been painted by Evangelist Luca. Initially, the shrine was just a tiny monastery (1192); the Church's construction began in 1194; then, it had been enlarged and restored from 1481 to the first decade of 1700. In 1433 Bologna was devastated by a torrential downpour with severe flood; an economic catastrophe of major proportions was about to take place. People were frightened and unable to cope but at the same time willing to find a solution. Believers proposed to carry the holy icon of the Virgin Mary to the centre, confident that she would have listened to their desperate prayers; while the Virgin was being carried the rain ceased.... a miracle had occurred. It was then decided that the icon would be transported to the city-centre every year. In fact, believers can visit the Virgin in "La Cattedrale di San Pietro" (St. Peter Cathedral) every May for five days. The long portico (3,5 Km) that leads to the shrine was designed by Antonio Conti in 1674; the portico features 666 arches in which one of them was placed a statue depicting *"Madonna col bambino"* (Madonna and her child). Between 1723 and 1774 the shrine underwent restoration under the direction of Dotti and his son; in 1756 the Church's facade was completed thanks to funds raised by Pope Benedict XVI, archbishop of Bologna.

VILLA ALDINI
(Via dell' Osservanza)

A villa rises on a hill called *"Colle dell' Osservanza"* (225m), which offers an impressive view of the town. Built in 1811 by Antonio Aldini, who was Napoleon's Minister, features a facade which recalls ancient Greek temples and a tiny Roman Church called "Madonna del Monte".

Villa Aldini, which recalls Greek Architecture

LA SCUOLA BOLOGNESE DELLA PITTURA
(BOLOGNESE SCHOOL OF PAINTING)

The 16th-17th-century school, which is rekoned to have been one of the most famous of the time, was founded by three gifted brothers: Carracci brothers; the eldest, *Ludovico*, was born in 1555, *Agostino,* who was born in 1557 and the youngst *Annibale*, born in 1560. Their family used to live in a very beautiful Palace located in the city centre between Via Rolandino and Via dei Poeti.

It has to be emphasised that Ludovico's lecturer was the well-known artist Tintoretto, from Venice. The youngest brother, Annibale, spent a lot of years in Rome where he met Caravaggio with whom he had worked on a project in Cerasi chapel (Cappella Cerasi); on his death Annibale

Ludovico Carracci's
"San Raimondo"

was buried close to Raffaello's grave in the Pantheon. After having studied the techniques of ancient artists and being extremely endowed with the art of painting, they decided to set up the school called *"L'Accademia degli Incamminati"*.

Guido Reni's "Il massacro degli innocenti"

Famous artists are believed to have attended the school: *Guido Reni* (1575-1642); he spent a few years in Rome and on his death was buried in Bologna in the "Basilica di San Domenico" in which his well-known fresco, *"Gloria dei Santi"*, is preserved.

Artists such as Francesco Albani and *Domenico Zampieri*, called *"il Domenichino"*, after having attended the school, they both moved to Rome and competed eagerly with Reni for the production of important frescos.

Giovanni Francesco Barbieri, called "il Guercino", who was born in 1591 and one of his masterpiece, "la Vestizione di San Guglielmo d'Aquitania", is kept in the National Art Gallery in Bologna (Pinacoteca Nazionale).

Eventually a great number of minor artists, who have contributed to increase the school's fame, attended the Bolognese School of Painting: *Lucio Massari* (1569-1633), *Giacomo Cavedoni* (1577-1660), *Alessandro Tiarini* (1577-1668), Leonello Spada (1576-1622), Carlo Cignani (1628-1719), Giuseppe Maria Crespi (1665-1747) and finally *Vittorio Maria Bigari* (1692-1776).

MUSEUMS AND GALLERIES

Museo Civico Archeologico - (Civic Museum of Archaeology)
Via dell'Archiginnasio, 2   Tel. 051 2757211
Opening hours: weekdays 9am-3pm;
Saturdays and public holidays: 10am.-6pm; closed on Mondays

The Museum was opened on September 25, 1881; the most dramatic archaeological discoveries of Prehistoric, Etruscan and Roman times are preserved in the building, as well as one of the most important European Egyptian Collections, thanks to the work of great archaeologists such as Ulisse Aldrovandi (1500) and Pier Ferdinando Marsili (1700). The Museum is located in a three floors building which once was a Hospital, "ex Ospedale della Morte"; the Egyptian Collection is placed in the basement, Roman and Greek sculptures are kept in the ground floor and finally archaeological discoveries of Etruscan Greek and Roman times are on the first floor.

Courtyard of the Museum of Archaeology

Following page:
Nero's bust exposed at the Museum
of Archaeology

Clear relief of Horembed Egypt tomb

Pinacoteca Nazionale
(National Picture Gallery)
Via Belle Arti, 56   Tel 051.4209411
Opening hours: weekdays 9am-1pm; closed on Mondays

In 1762 the Institute, founded by Marsigli, was given some paintings belonging to the first decade of 1500; later, in 1776 14 th-century paintings were added as well; as the power of the Church began to fall apart, hundreds of paintings had been transported from Churches to the Gallery. Not until Napoleon Empire had fallen apart and the number of works of Art available dramatically increased was the building eventually opened to the public (1875); in 1884 five hundreds more works were added to the collection. The latest restoration of the building was done in 1960; the *"Pinacoteca"* is divide into twenty-nine halls and holds paintings from: *"I pittori Primitivi"*: Francesco Cossa, Lorenzo Costa, Ercole dè Roberti, Francesco Francia, Raffaello Sanzio, Amico Aspertini, il Perugino, Nicolò Pisano, il Parmigianino, Pellegrino Tibaldi, Tintoretto and Tiziano.

National Picture Gallery: Raffaello's painting "Estasi di Santa Cecilia"

National Picture Gallery: detail of Vitale da Bologna's painting "Storie di Santo Antonio"

"Il Manierismo": Bsrtolomeo Passerotti, Prospero Fontana and Bartolomeo Cesi. *"I Carracci"*: Ludovico, Annibale Agostino Carracci and Guido Reni. *"L'età Barocca and 700"*: Domenichino, A. Tiarini, Guercino, Elisabetta Sirani, Donato Creti and Luigi Crespi.

Collezioni Comunali d'Arte di Bologna
(Bologna Art Collections)
Piazza Maggiore 6   Tel 051.2193998
Opening hours: 9am-6pm; closed on Mondays

A dramatic collection of works of Art is kept on the second floor of the Communal Palace, which was the residence of Cardinal Legato (1859). The floor, divided into eighteen halls, preserves paintings of Palagi, Baruzzi, Pepoli, Pizzardi, Verzaglia and Pier Ignazio Rusconi; besides this, it is possible to appreciate sculptures and silverware by great artists (1400-1800) such as Vitale da Bologna, Jacopo di Paolo, Giunta Pisano, Francesco Francia, Jacopo Tintoretto, Giuseppe Maria Crespi, Donato Creti and Luca Signorelli.

Great Staircase leading to the Art Collection Halls

Interior of one of the Art Collection Halls

Biblioteca Comunale dell'Archiginnasio
(Archiginnasio Municipal Library)
Piazza Galvani 1   Tel 051.276811
Opening hours: 9am-1pm; closed on public holidays

It is reckoned to be one of the greatest libraries throughout Italy and preserve more than 700,000 volumes, prints and other material.

Museo Morandi
(Morandi Museum)
Via Don Minzoni, 14   Tel. 051.6496611
Opening hours: 12am-6am; closed on Mondays

Two hundred and sixty-three works of Art of Morandi are kept in the Museum.

Museo Civico Medievale
(Medieval Civic Museum)
Via Manzoni, 4   tel. 051.2193930
Opening hours: weekdays 9am-3pm;
Public holidays: 10am-6pm; closed on Tuesdays

The Museum features a great collection of weapons, Medieval sculptures and tombs.

Museo Civico d'Arte Industriale e
Galleria Davia Bargellini
(Industrial Art Museum and Davia Bargellini Gallery)
Strada Maggiore, 44   tel. 051.236708
Opening hours: 9am-2pm; Sundays: 9am-1pm; closed on Mondays
and on weekday public holidays

The Museum, which was opened in 1924 thanks to Francesco Malaguzzi, preserves beautiful and interesting objects of skilful artisans; on the other hand, works of Art to honour Bargellini family, such as "*Madonna dei denti*" by Vitale da Bologna, are kept in the Gallery.

Museo Civico del Risorgimento
(Italian 1st and 2nd Risorgimento Civic Museum)
Piazza Carducci 5   tel. 051.347592
Opening hours: 9am-1pm; closed on Mondays and weekday public
holidays.

Originally the Museum was an oratory, "Oratorio della Madonna del Piombo", and later became the residence of the great Italian poet Giosuè Carducci. A collection of weapons, prints and military

Davia Bargellini Museum: the ancient puppet theatre

uniforms are preserved in the building.

Museo Civico Bibliografico Musicale
(Bibliography Cvic Museum on music works)
Strada Maggiore 34 Tel. 051.2757711
Opening hours: 9am-4pm; closed on Sundays and on weekday public holidays.

The Museum is located close to the Academy of Music G.B. Martini and preserves more than 20,000 works of music as well as many portraits of famous artists. The Museum is reckoned to have the unique original copy of "*Harmonicae Museces Odhecaton*" by Ottaviano Petrucci (1501).

Galleria d'Arte Moderna - Mambo
(Modern Art Gallery)
Via Don Minzoni, 14   Tel. 051.6496611
Opening hours: from 12am to 6pm and from 3pm to 7pm;
closed on Mondays

Preserves works of Art of 19th and 20th-century artists from Bologna and Emilia.

Museo del Patrimonio Industriale
(Industrial Property Museum)
Via della Beverara, 123   tel. 051.6356611
Opening hours: Tuesdays-Wednesdays-Fridays-Saturdays:
9.30am-12.30am; Thursdays and Saturdays: 2.30pm-5.30pm;
closed on Mondays and on public holidays

The Museum preserves industrial machinery and gives information about the evolution of industrial technology

Museo Storico Didattico della Tappezzeria
(Historical Museum of Tapestries)
Via Casaglia, 3   Tel 051.6145512
Opening hours: 9am-1pm; closed on Mondays and on weekday
public holidays.

The Museum was opened in 1966 by Vittorio Zironi and is reckoned to have a stunning collection of 6,000 tapestries from all over the world and an exhibition of working machinery.

*Ancient tapestry
exhibited at the Museum
of Tapestries*

Museo Nazionale del Soldatino
(National Museum of toy soldiers in miniature)
Via Toscana, 19   tel. 051.266836
Opening hours: 9am to 1pm

The Museum is located in Villa Aldrovandi Mazzacorati and preserves more than 14,500 miniatures of toy soldier from the 1800 to present times.

CHURCH'S MUSEUMS

Museo di Santo Stefano-Piazza Santo Stefano-Tel. 051.223256
Museo di San Domenico-Piazza San Domenico- Tel.051.6400411
Museo di San Petronio-Piazza Maggiore-Tel. 051.231415
Museo della Santa-Via Tagliapietre, 19-Tel. 051.331277
Museo Missionario d'Arte Cinese
Via dell'Osservanza, 88 - Tel. 051.580597

UNIVERSITY'S MUSEUMS
Via Zamboni, 33- Information desk from 9am to 1pm
Tel. 051.2099360

*Musei di Palazzo Poggi-*Via Zamboni,33 - Tel. 051.2099398
Museo Storico dello Studio-Aula Carducci
Museo delle Navi
Museo Ostetrico G.A.Galli
Museo di Architettura Militare
Museo Indiano
Specola e Museo d'Astronomia
Opening hours: weekdays from 10am to 13pm

Museo di Zoologia
(Museum of Zoology)
Via Selmi, 3   tel. 051.2094248
Opening hours: from 9am to 6pm

Museo di Anatomia Comparata
(Museum of Anatomy)
Via Selmi 3   tel. 051.2099140
Opening hours:from 9am to 1 pm

Museo di Antropologia
(Museum of Anthropology)
Via Selmi, 3   tel. 051.2094195
Opening hours: from 9am to 1pm

Orto Botanico-Erbario
(Botanical Gardens)
Via Irnerio 42 tel. 051.2091304
Opening hours: from 9am to 1pm

Museo di Fisica
(Museum of Physics)
Via Irnerio, 46 tel. 051.2091099
Opening hours: from 9am to 1 pm

Museo di Geologia e Paleontologia
(Museum of Geology and Palaeontology)
Via Zamboni, 63 tel. 051.2094555
Opening hours:from 9am to 1 pm

Museo di Mineralogia e Petrografia
(Museum of Mineralogy)
Piazza di Porta San Donato, 1 tel. 051.2094926
Opening hours: from 9am to 1pm

Museo di Anatomia degli Animali Domestici
con Istologia ed Imbriologia
(Museum of pet's Anatomy Histology and Embryology)
Via Tolara di Sotto - Ozzano Emilia   tel. 051.2097996
Opening hours: whenever required

Museo di Patologia Generale e Anatomia Patologica
Veterinaria
(Museum of general Pathology and Veterinary Anatomical
Pathology)
Via Tolara di Sotto - Ozzano Emilia   tel. 051.2097000
Opening hours:whenever required

Museo di Anatomia e Istologia Patologica
(Museum of Anatomy and Pathological Histology)
Via Massarenti, 9 tel. 051.391540
Opening hours: whenever required

EXCITING DISHES FOR CREATIVE CUISINE

We would like to propose some of the characteristic dishes that you can try in lovely restaurants in town.

Bolognese meat sauce
Ingredients for 6 persons: 500 grams of meat, either veal or beef, 100 grams of bacon, 1 onion, 1 celery, 1 carrot finely chopped; half glass of white wine, 300 grams of tomato sauce, 50 grams of butter, 1/2 tsp salt and 1/2 tsp pepper and 2 tsp of oil.

Fry vegetables in butter and oil; add chopped bacon and meat; lower heat to minimum, add half glass of wine and as soon as the wine evaporates add pepper, salt and the tomato sauce. If you like a richer sauce, add some chicken livers and mushrooms, provided that they have previously been slightly fried.

Tortellini alla Bolognese

This is certainly one of the most famous dishes of Bologna;
Ingredients for 6 persons: 100 grams of pork, 100 grams of
turkey breasts, 150 grams of raw ham, 100 grams of Italian
mortadella, 150 grams of parmesan cheese, 2 eggs, 1/2 tsp salt,
1/2 tsp pepper, grated fresh nutmeg.

Beat the meat with a meat mallet to flatten it then cut into thin
slices and mix with row ham and mortadella finely cut. Add the
parmesan cheese, eggs, salt, pepper and nutmeg; place it in
large bowl and leave the mixture for about 2-3 hours. For the
pastry: 400 grams of plain flour and 4 eggs, a half glass of
warm water, 50 grams of butter. Add the butter and salt to the
flour and rub in well. Mix to a soft dough with the water and
knead until the dough feels soft and velvety. Divide the dough
into 4-5 cm long squares and pour a teaspoon of the filling in
the centre of each square. Roll out each square to a triangle
pressing the edges and finally wrap each triangle around your
finger and overlap the two ends. Each piece will form a "tortellino". Boil them in a nice meat consommé and serve hot with
lots of grated parmesan cheese.

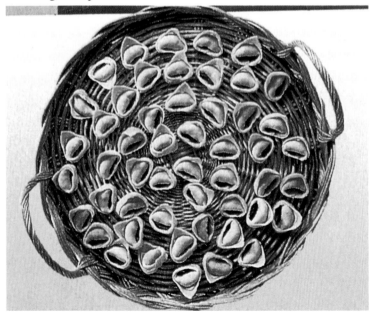

Cotolette alla Bolognese

Ingredients for 6 persons: 6 thin veal slices, 50 grams of butter, 1 slice of raw ham for each slice of meat, 1 tablespoon of tomato sauce, 300 grams of bread crumbs and 3 eggs.

Mix each slice with eggs and bread crumbles, then press them down gently; fry at low heat in melted butter and place them in a baking-pan. Add raw ham on each slice, add slivers of cheese and moisten them with 1 tablespoon of tomato sauce. Cook at a low heat until cheese melts.

Tagliatelle Verdi

This one of the typical dishes of Bolognese cooking.

Ingredients for 6 persons: 200 grams of spinach, previously boiled; 600 grams of plain flour, 4 eggs.

Mix flour, eggs and spinach; rub in well and mix to a soft dough. Leave the dough to dry for a few hours; then divide the dough into 1/2 cm large strips. Cover the pasta with a towel to prevent them from get dried; boil them in salted water and flavour them either with meat sauce or melted butter and parmesan cheese.

Gnocco Fritto

Ingredients: 500 grams of plain flour, 40 grams of lard, 40 grams of yeast, 1/2 tsp bicarbonate, 1/2 tsp salt and a half glass of finger warmed milk.

Add all the ingredients to the flour and rub in well to a soft velvety dough; cover the dough with a towel and leave for 1 hour; then, roll the dough, divide it into rhombuses and fry with lard. "Gnocco Fritto" should be eaten warm with soft cheese and ham.

Punta di vitello al forno

Ingredients for 6 persons: 1kg of boned veal breast, 50 grams of lard, 1/2 tsp pepper, 1/2 onions ,1 carrot, 1 celery and 1 sprig of parsley all finely chopped in 50 grams of butter, a bit of rosemary.
Mix all the dry ingredients into a large bowl; add the meat and place everything in a baking-pan. Bake in hot oven for about 1 hour and a half; you can add white wine. Serve it either hot or cold.

La Spongata

This is reckoned to be one of the most ancient fruit cake of Bologna traditional cooking.

Recipe:

100 grams of peeled and roasted almonds, 50 grams of sugar; heat 250 grams of honey in a pan and when it starts to melt add 100 grams of peeled hazelnuts, 100 grams of chopped walnut kernels, 1 tsp almond powder, 150 grams of dried grated biscuits, 1 grated nutmeg, 1/2 tsp cinnamon powder and 1/2 tsp of pepper.

Stir the ingredients well and then remove the pan from heat; when the pan is cold, add 150 grams of candied peel, 50 grams of pine-nuts and 100 grams of raisins. Leave the mixture for a day;

For the pastry: 400 grams of plain flour, 100 grams of sugar, 120 grams of butter, 1/2 tsp salt and enough white wine to get a rather solid dough.

Mix all the ingredients and rub in well; divide the dough into a lot of layers and fill each layer with

some of the filling; put the layers one on top of the others, moisten the top edges and seal. Place the mixture in a buttered baking-pan in hot oven for about 30 minutes.

Torta di Riso

This rice cake is also called "alla petroniana".
Recipe:
boil 100 grams of rice in 1 litre of milk; cut in small pieces 100 grams of almonds and 100 grams of candy citron. Mix 6 eggs with 280 grams of sugar and 50 grams of vanilla and add almonds, candy citron and a glass of "amaretto" liqueur. Stir the mixture in the cold rice, place everything in a buttered pan and leave the filling in hot oven for 40 minutes.

BOLOGNA EXHIBITIONS
Call 051.282111 for accurate information
www.bolognafiere.it

January
Marca by Bologna Fiere • Arte Fiera

February
ForumClub Forumpiscine • Saie3 • Biennale T3

March
**Saie3 • Biennale3 • Cosmopack • Cosmoprof World Wide
Il mondo Creativo Spring • Mondo Elettronica
Bologna Children's Book Fair
Bologna Licensing Trade Fair**

April
**Linea pelle • Alma orienta • Univercity • Expo pixel
Pharmintech • Cosmofarma Exhibition**

May
Zoomark International • PTE Expo • Autopromotec

June
**R2b - Research To Business
Smau Bologna • Music Italy Show • The Jambo**

September
Sana • Cersaie

October
**Simac • Tanning-Tech • Linea Pelle • Saie
Smart City Exhibition
Ambiente Lavoro
Expo Tunnel**

November
**Fishing Show • Il Mondo Creativo
Model game • The Cake Show • Big Buyer**

December
Motor Show

HOTELS

★★★★★L
Grand Hotel Majestic Baglioni - Via Indipendenza 8 - tel. 051 225445
★★★★
Abitalia - via Masini 4 - tel. 051 242811
AC - via S. Serlio 28 - tel. 051 377246
Aemilia - via Z. Alvisi 8 - tel. 051 3940311
Al Cappello Rosso - via dè Fusari 9 - tel. 051 261891
Amadeus - via M.E. Lepido 39 - tel. 051403040
Best Western City - via Magenta 10 - tel. 051 372676
B4 Bologna Tower - via Lenin 43 - tel. 051 60205555
Corona d'Oro Art Hotel - via Oberdan 12 - tel. 051 7457611
Commercianti Art Hotel - via Pignattari 11 - tel. 051 7457511
Cosmopolitan - via Commercio Associato 9 - tel. 051 6926403
Ega - via Indipendenza 60 - tel. 051 245483
Europa Zanhotel - via Boidrini 11 - tel. 051 4211348
Express By Holiday Inn Fiera - via Commercio Associato 3 - tel. 051 6334588
HC3 - via Arcoveggio 46 - tel. 051 866 248 5388
H.M.C. Le Drapperie - via Drapperie 5 - tel. 051 223955
I Portici - via Indipendenza 69 - tel. 051 4218511
My One - via Togliatti 11 - tel. 051 4380027
NH De La Gare - p.zza XX Settembre 2 - tel. 051 281611
Novecento Art Hotel - p.zza Galileo 4/3 - tel. 051 7457311
Novotel Fiera - via Michelino 23 - tel. 051 519224
Ramada Encore - via Ferrarese 164 - tel. 051 4161311
Royal H. Carlton - via Montebello 8 - tel. 051 249361
Savhotel - via F. Parri 9 - tel. 051 361361
Savoia Country House - via San Donato 159 - tel. 051 6332366
Savoia Regency - via del Pilastro 2 - tel. 051 512635
Sheraton Bologna - via Aeroporto 34 - tel. 051 400056
Starhotel Excelsior - viale Pietramellara 51 - tel. 051 246178
Suite Hotel Elite - via Saffi 36 - tel. 6459011
Tre Vecchi Zanhotel - via Indipendenza 47 - tel. 051 231991
Una Hotel - viale Pietramellara 41 - tel. 051 60801
Unaway - p.zza Costituzione - tel. 05141666
★★★
Alloro Suite - via Ferrarese 161 - tel. 051 342127
Astor - via Fioravanti 42/2 - tel. 051 356663
Astoria - via F.lli Rosselli 14 - tel. 051 521410
Best Western Maggiore - via Emilia Ponente 62 - tel. 051 381634
Biocasamia - via Marconi 45 - tel. 051 6486462

Blumen - via Mazzini 45 - tel. 05l 344672
Cavour - via Goito 4 - tel. 051 228111
Centro Turistico Città di Bologna - via Romita 12 - tel. 051325016
Corticella - via Stoppato 31 - tel. 051 324701
CR.IS.MA - via Ferrarese 164 - tel. 051 325076
De La Ville - viale XII Giugno 7 - tel. 051 582243
Donatello - via Indipendenza 65 - tel. 051 248174
Due Torri - via degli Usberti 4 - tel. 051 239944
Fiera - via Stalingrado 82 - tel. 051377735
Il Canale Zanhotel - via Bertiera 2 - tel. 051 222098
Il Guercino - via L. Serra 7 - tel. 051 369893
La Pioppa - via M. E. Lepido 217 - tel. 051400234
Mapri - via Z. Alvisi 20 - tel. 051 343678
Marco Polo - via M. Polo 89/a - tel. 051 6340050
Maxim - via Stalingrado 152 - tel. 051 323235
Metropolitan - via dell'Orso 4 - tel. 051 229393
Nuovo H. Del Porto - via del Porto 6 - tel. 051 247926
Orologio Art Hotel - via IV Novembre 10 - tel. 051 231253
Palace - via Montegrappa 2 - tel. 051 237442
Paradise - vic. Cattani 7 - tel. 051 231792
Porta San Mamolo - via Falcone 6/b - tel. 051 583056
Re Enzo - via S. Croce 26 - tel. 051 523322
Regina Zanhotel - via Indipendenza 51 - tel. 051 248878
Roma - via D'Azeglio 9 - tel. 051 231330
San Felice - via Riva Reno 2 - tel. 051 557457
Sterlino - via Murri 71 - tel. 051 342751
Suite - via del Gomito 16 - tel. 051 327183
Top Park - via Toscana 67 - tel. 051 6516504
Touring - via dè Mattuiani 1/2 - tel. 051 330486
University - via Mentana 7 - tel. 051229713
★★
Accademia - via Belle Arti 6 - tel. 051 232318
A.G.A.R.F. - via Mattei 72 - tel. 051 532118
Arcoveggio - via L: Spada 27 - tel. 051 355436
Atlantic - via Galliera 46 - tel. 051 248488
Centrale - via della Zecca 2 - tel. 051 225114
Conte Luna - via Benazza 6 - tel. 051 6344994
Maini Cacciari Marconi - via Marconi 22 - tel. 051 262832
Navile - via Sostegno 13 - tel. 051 6340394
Orsi - via Pastrengo 3 - tel. 051 7414399
San Giorgio - via delle Moline 17 - tel. 051 248659
Tuscolano - via del Tuscolano 29 - tel. 051324024

★

Bologna - via Massarentì 98 - tel. 051 304664
Cesari Cotti Pedrini - Strada Maggiore 79 - tel. 051 300081
Garisenda - Galleria Leone 1 - tel. 051 224369
Giardinetto - via Massarenti 76 - tel. 051 342793
Ideale - via Sirani 5 - tel. 051 358270
Pallone - via del Pallone 4 - tel. 051 4210533
Perla - via San Vitale 77/2 - tel. 051 224579
S. Orsola - via Palmieri 25 - tel. 051 302997
San Vitale - via S. Vitale 94 - tel. 051 225966
Villa Azzurra - viale Felsina 49 - tel. 051501348

CINEMA DI BOLOGNA

Alba - via dell'Arcoveggio, 3 - tel. 051 352906
Antoniano - via Guinizzelli, 3 - tel. 051 3940212
Arlecchino - via delle Lame, 57 - tel. 051 522285
Bellinzona - via Bellinzona, 6 - tel. 051 6446940
Bristol - via Toscana, 146 - tel. 051 474015
Capitol Multisala - via Milazzo, 1 - tel. 051 241002
Chaplin - piazza di porta Saragozza, 5 - tel. 051 585253
Europa - via Pietralata, 55 - tel. 051 523812
Fossolo - via Lincoln, 3 - tel 051 540114
Galliera - via Matteotti, 25 - tel. 051 4151762
Jolly - via Marconi, 14 - tel. 051 224505
Lumière - via Azzo Gardino, 85 - tel. 051 2195311
Medica Palace - via Monte Grappa, 9 - tel. 051 221362
Nuovo Nosadella - via Berti, 2 - tel. 051 521550
Odeon Multisala - via Mascarella, 3 - tel. 051 227916
Orione - via Cimabue, 14 - tel. 051 382403
Perla - via San Donato, 34 - tel. 051 242212
Rialto Studio - via Rialto, 19 - tel. 051 227926
Roma d'Essai - via Fondazza, 4 - tel. 051 347470
Smeraldo - via Toscana, 125 - tel. 051 473959
The Space Multisala - via Europa, 5 - tel. 051 892111
Tivoli - via Massarenti, 418 - tel. 051 532417

THEATRE

Arena del Sole - via Indipendenza 44 - tel. 051.2910910
Bibiena - via San Vitale 13 - tel. 051.228291
Comunale - largo Respighi 1 - tel. 051.529011
Dehon - via Libia 59 - tel. 051.342934
Delle Celebrazioni - via Saragozza, 234 - tel. 051.6153370
Di Leo - via San Vitale 63 - tel. 051.227108
Duse - via Cartoleria 42 - tel. 051.231836
Europa Auditorium - piazza Costituzione 4 - tel. 051.372540
San Martino - via Oberdan 25 - tel. 051.224671
Testoni - via Matteotti 16 - tel. 051.4153800

CAR PARKS IN THE CITY CENTRE
(parking meters indicate parking areas)

Viale Silvani - 200 parking lots
Via L.Calori - 100 parking lots
Via del Rondone - 100 parking lots
Via F.lli Cairoli - 100 parking lots
Via Azzogardino - 100 parking lots
Via Riva di Reno - 150 parking lots
Piazza XX Settembre - 150 parking lots
Piazza XX Settembre - 520 parking lots
Via Gramsci - 120 parking lots
Via Monte Grappa - 150 parking lots
Piazza VIII Agosto - 490 parking lots
Piazza F. D. Roosvelt - 300 parking lots
Piazza G. Carducci - 200 parking lots
Via Caracci - 410 parking lots
Ex Staveco - Viale Panzacchi - 170parking lots
Fiera District - 200 posti
Piazza VIII Agosto - 1000 parking lots
Piazza Azzarita - parking lots

BUS SERVICES TO MAIN DESTINATIONS

Aeroporto G.Marconi: Aerobus 91
(Airport G.Marconi)
Autostazione Corriere: 11 17 27 30 32 33 36 37 38 39 50 87
(Coaches Station)   91 92 95 97 98
Comune di Bologna: 11 13 14 17 18 19 20 25 27 29
Fiera District: 18 21 34 35 38 39 88 91
(Exhibition area)
Galleria d'Arte Moderna: 18 35 38 39 91
(Modern Art Gallery)
Giardini Margherita: 13 17 30 32 33 38 39 50 90 96
(Giardini Margherita Park)
Ippodromo Arcoveggio: 12 27 97 98
(Racecourse)
Ospedale Bellaria: 90
(Hospital)
Ospedale Maggiore: 13 19 35 38 39 87 91 92 93 96 Aerobus
(Hospital)
Ospedale Rizzoli: 30
(Hospital)
Ospedale Sant'Orsola: 14 19 25 27 36 89 94
(Hospital)
Ospedale Malpighi: 25 34 36 94
(Hospital)
Palazzo dello Sport: 13 18 19 36 38 39 87 91 92 93 96
(Sport Centre)
Palazzo dei Congressi: 18 35 38 91
(Conference Centre)
Pinacoteca Nazionale: 20 32 33 36 37
(National Picture Gallery)
Provincia di Bologna: 14 18 19 25 27 50
Questura Centrale: 11 13 14 17 18 19 20 25 27 29 30 87 90 96
(Police Station)
Stadio Comunale: 14 20 21 37 38 39 89 94
(Stadium)
Stazione Centrale FS: 17 21 25 30 32 33 35 36 37 38 39 50 90
(Railway Station)   91 98 Areobus
Teatro Comunale: 50
(Theatre)
Università: 20 32 33 36 37 50 89 93 94
(University)

PRACTICAL TIPS
Poste Code 40100

Tourist Information Offices: Piazza Maggiore, 1/E
tel. 051.239660

Taxi - CAT tel. 051.4590 - COTABO tel. 051.372727
Emergencies
A.C.I. soccorso stradale - tel. 803116
Carabinieri - tel.112
Ambulance - tel. 118
Police - 051.526911
Fire Service - tel.1515 - www.comune.bologna.it/iperbole/vvfbo
Pronto Intervento P.S. - tel. 113

International Airport G.Marconi (Borgo Panigale)
www.bologna-airport.it
Information - tel. 051.6479615   Luggage - tel. 051.6472076
Bus piazza XX Settembre - tel. 051.245400
www.autostazionebo.it

Railway Station Trenitalia - Information tel. 051.892021
www.trenitalia.com

Exhibitions information office - viale della Fiera 20
tel. 051.282111 - www.bolognafiere.it
Racecourse via di Corticella 184 - tel. 051.3540311
www.rokeby.com/cesenate/arcoveggio.html

Hospitals
Bellaria - via Altura 3 - tel. 051.6225111
Sant'Orsola - via Massarenti 9 - tel. 051.6363111 - www.aosp.bo.it
Malpighi - via Albertoni 15 - tel. 051.6361111
Maggiore - via Nigrisoli 2 - tel. 051.6478111
Rizzoli - via Pupilli, 1 - tel. 051.6366111 - www.ior.it

Palazzo dei Congressi - piazza Costituzione 6/c - tel. 051.6375111
(Congress Palace)
Palazzo dello Sport - piazza Azzarita 8 - tel. 051.557283
(Sport Centre)
Polizia Municipale - via Enzo Ferrari 42 - tel. 051.266626
Stadium - via De Coubertin - tel. 411651